Basic Astronomy Concepts
Everyone Should Know
(with Space Photos)

   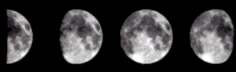

Chris McMullen, Ph.D.
Northwestern State University of Louisiana

Like Explaining the Phases of the Moon and Evidence for the Heliocentric Theory

Basic Astronomy Concepts Everyone Should Know (with Space Photos).
Like Explaining the Phases of the Moon and Evidence for the Heliocentric Theory.

Astro Nutz.

Chris McMullen, Ph.D.
Northwestern State University of Louisiana.

CONTENTS

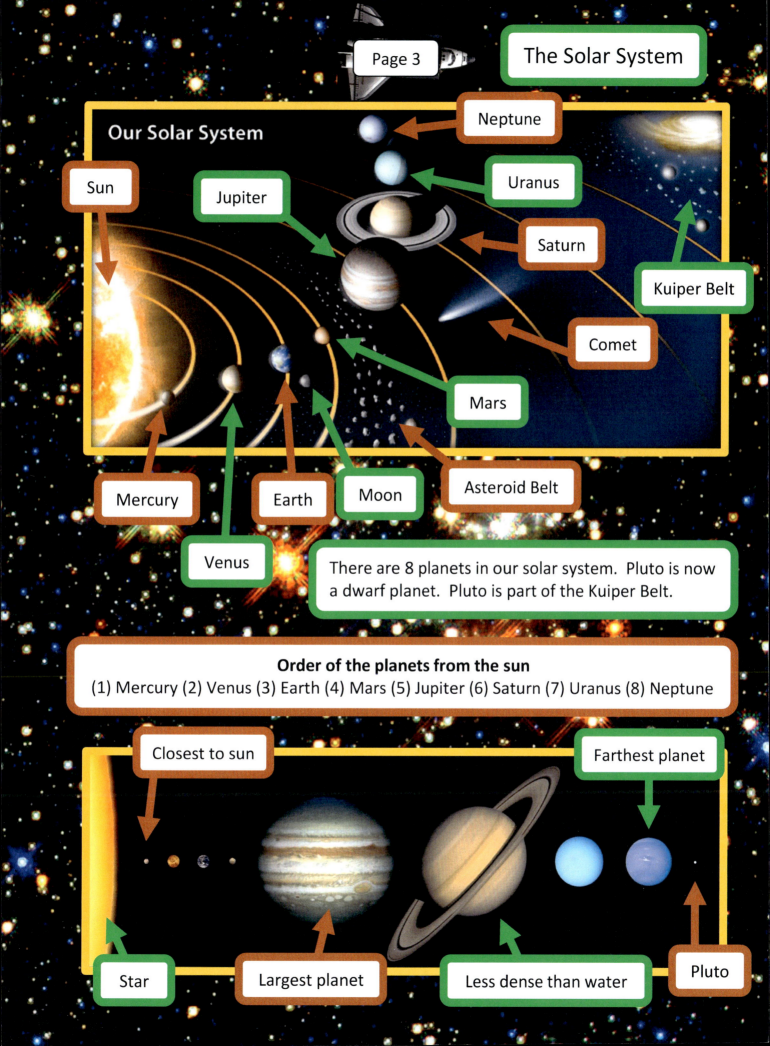

The Solar System

Our Solar System

Neptune

Uranus

Saturn

Kuiper Belt

Comet

Sun

Jupiter

Mars

Mercury

Earth

Moon

Asteroid Belt

Venus

There are 8 planets in our solar system. Pluto is now a dwarf planet. Pluto is part of the Kuiper Belt.

Order of the planets from the sun
(1) Mercury (2) Venus (3) Earth (4) Mars (5) Jupiter (6) Saturn (7) Uranus (8) Neptune

Closest to sun

Farthest planet

Star

Largest planet

Less dense than water

Pluto

The Sun

Don't look directly at the sun because direct sunlight has enough intensity to permanently damage your eye in very little time; it can burn out your retinas in minutes, and do very serious damage in much less time.

Surface temperature: 5800 K
That's 2000 K more than the melting point of any metal!
Composition: H, He

Radius: $108\ R_E$
(R_E = earth's radius)
Mass: $333{,}000\ M_E$
(M_E = earth's mass)
Density: 1.4 g/cc
(compare to water, 1 g/cc)

The ultraviolet (UV) photos of the sun shown here show the solar activity that is constantly occurring near its surface.

Mercury has the most extreme day/night temperature variations. It is 700 Kelvin during the day (that's much hotter than boiling water), but only 100 Kelvin at night (that's about 200 K colder than the freezing point of water).

Density: 5.4 g/cc
1 'year': 88 earth days
1 'day': 59 earth days
Axis tilt: 0°
Made of rocks, metals
0 moons, 0 rings

Orbital radius: 0.4 AU
(1 AU = earth's orb. rad.)
Radius: $0.4\ R_E$
Mass: $0.055\ M_E$
Surface temperature:
700 K (day), 100 K (night)

Mercury has virtually no atmosphere. Mercury is heavily cratered, like the moon, because it has a very thin atmosphere and is geologically inactive.

Venus

Venus rotates backwards on its axis.

Venus has the hottest average surface temperature – 740 K. The reason for this is that Venus has an extreme greenhouse effect (trapped solar radiation that warms a planet's surface and cools its atmosphere).

Orbital radius: 0.7 AU
Radius: $0.95\ R_E$
Mass: $0.82\ M_E$
Surface temperature: 740 K
Density: 5.2 g/cc

1 'year': 225 earth days
1 'day': 243 earth days
Axis tilt: 177°
Made of rocks, metals
0 moons, 0 rings

Venus is always covered with clouds. The pictures that we have of Venus either show its clouds or use radar to produce an image of the surface beneath the clouds, except for close-up images of the surface taken by landing spacecraft.

Earth

Water covers 71% of earth's surface.

1 'year': 365 earth days
1 'day': 24 earth hours
Axis tilt: 23.5°
Made of rocks, metals
1 moon, 0 rings

In 1969, Neil Armstrong became the first person to walk on the moon. Neil Armstrong and Buzz Aldrin walked on the moon that day as part of NASA's Apollo 11 mission.

Orbital radius: 1.0 AU
Radius: $1.0\ R_E$
Mass: $1.0\ M_E$
Surface temperature: 290 K
Density: 5.5 g/cc

The moon has very little atmosphere and is geologically inactive. Its surface is heavily cratered. However, there are large regions that are smooth, which appear dark in the photo to the right. We call these maria, which means seas. (Mare is singular, maria is plural.)

Mars

Mars has two moons, named Phobos (Foe-bus) and Deimos (Die-mus), which are very small. Phobos, the larger of the two moons, is shown above.

Orbital radius: 1.5 AU
Radius: 0.53 R_E
Mass: 0.11 M_E
Surface temperature: 220 K
Density: 3.9 g/cc

1 'year': 1.9 earth yrs
1 'day': 24.6 earth hrs
Axis tilt: 25.2°
Made of rocks, metals
2 moons, 0 rings

The polar ice caps on Mars contain both dry ice (frozen carbon dioxide) and ice (frozen water). Examination of the geographic features of Mars – such as dried riverbeds – shows that Mars had liquid water in its distant past.

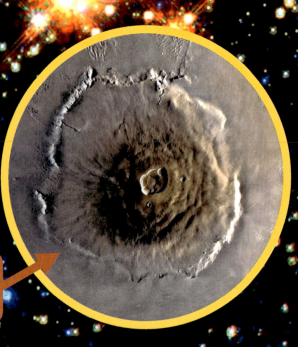

Mars has the largest volcano (Olympus Mons).

Jupiter

Jupiter is the largest planet.

1 'year': 11.9 earth yrs
1 'day': 9.9 earth hrs
Axis tilt: 3.1°
Composition: H, He
rings, 63+ moons

The most famous feature of Jupiter is the Great Red Spot. The Great Red Spot, visible in the photo above and enlarged in the photo below, is a very large hurricane (about twice as large as Earth) in Jupiter's atmosphere, which has existed for at least a couple of hundred years.

Orbital radius: 5.2 AU
Radius: 11.2 R_E
Mass: 318 M_E
Surface temperature: 125 K
Density: 1.3 g/cc

Europa (You-row-puh) Io (Eye-oh)

Callisto (Kuh-lis-toe)

Ganymede (Gan-i-mead)

The four largest moons of Jupiter are Ganymede (Gan-i-mead), Callisto (Kuh-lis-toe), Io (Eye-oh), and Europa (You-row-puh). Ganymede is the largest moon in our solar system. Io's surface has active volcanoes all over it. Europa's surface is icy. Callisto is a giant ball of ice with craters.

Saturn

Titan is Saturn's largest moon.

One 'year': 29.4 earth yrs
One 'day': 10.6 earth hrs
Axis tilt: 26.7°
Composition: H, He
rings, 60+ moons

Orbital radius: 9.5 AU
Radius: 9.4 R_E
Mass: 95 M_E
Surface temperature: 95 K
Density: 0.7 g/cc
(less dense than water!)

Saturn has the most prominent rings, which are actually composed of numerous chunks of ice and rocks.

Uranus

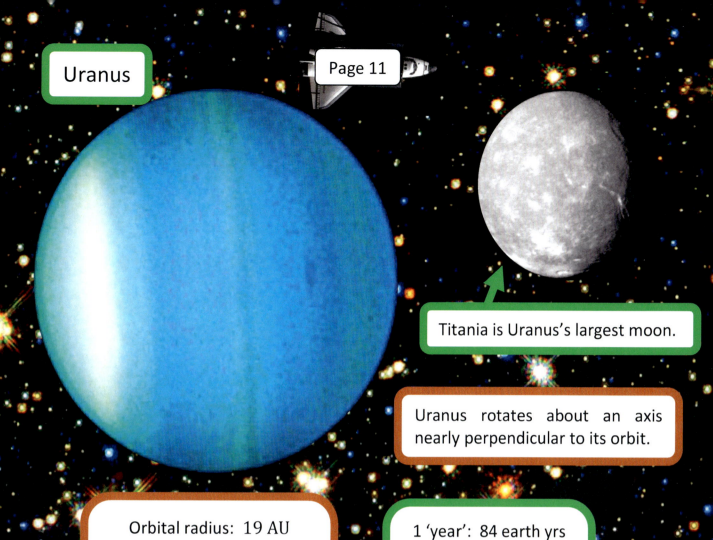

Titania is Uranus's largest moon.

Uranus rotates about an axis nearly perpendicular to its orbit.

Orbital radius: 19 AU
Radius: $4.0\ R_E$
Mass: $15\ M_E$
Surface temperature: 60 K
Density: 1.3 g/cc

1 'year': 84 earth yrs
1 'day': 17 earth hrs
Axis tilt: 97.9°
Composition: H/He
Rings, 27+ moons

Uranus has 5 large moons: Titania, Oberon, Umbriel, Ariel, and Miranda. Titania is the largest of Uranus's moons, and is only slightly larger than Oberon.

Neptune

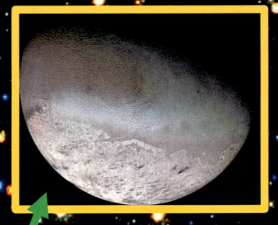

Triton is Neptune's largest moon.

Neptune is the most distant planet now that Pluto has been classified as a dwarf planet.

Orbital radius: 30 AU
Radius: 3.9 R_E
Mass: 17 M_E
Surface temperature: 60 K
Density: 1.6 g/cc

1 'year': 165 earth yrs
1 'day': 16 earth hrs
Axis tilt: 29.6°
Composition: H/He
Rings, 13+ moons

Triton is the only moon in our solar system to orbit its planet backwards compared to all of the others.

The gap between the orbits of Uranus and Neptune is greater than the gap between the orbits of any other two consecutive planets.

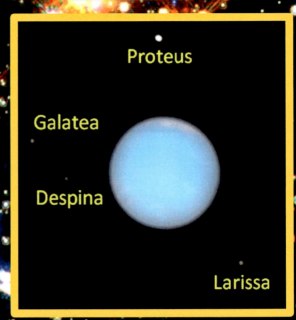

Proteus

Galatea

Despina

Larissa

Largest known Kuiper Belt objects

"Gabrielle"

"Xena"
(2003 UB313)

Pluto

Charon

2005 FY9

2003 EL61

Sedna

Quaoar

Why is Pluto a dwarf planet now, instead of a planet? Pluto is part of a belt that consists of countless icy bodies – whereas what we consider to be planets have enough mass that they clear out most of the other matter in their orbital neighborhood. Pluto is similar to comets and other icy objects in the Kuiper Belt – it isn't a gas giant like the outer planets. Finally, Pluto has a highly elliptical orbit, and its orbit is significantly tilted relative to the plane of the solar system.

The largest known Kuiper Belt object, Eris, is not shown in the top figure.

The two largest known Kuiper Belt objects are the dwarf planets Eris (Ee-ris) and Pluto.

Moon

Eris

Ceres

Pluto

Charon

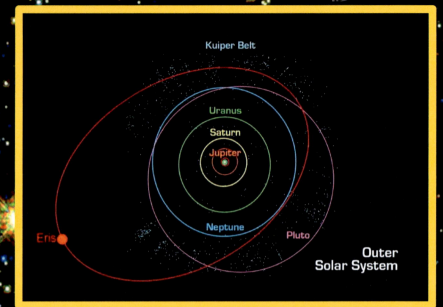

Numerous icy bodies reside in a large belt beyond Neptune called the Kuiper (Kie-per) Belt.

Beyond the Kuiper Belt lies the Oort (Ort) Cloud. The Oort Cloud is a sparse region of space that extends beyond the Kuiper Belt to the edge of our solar system.

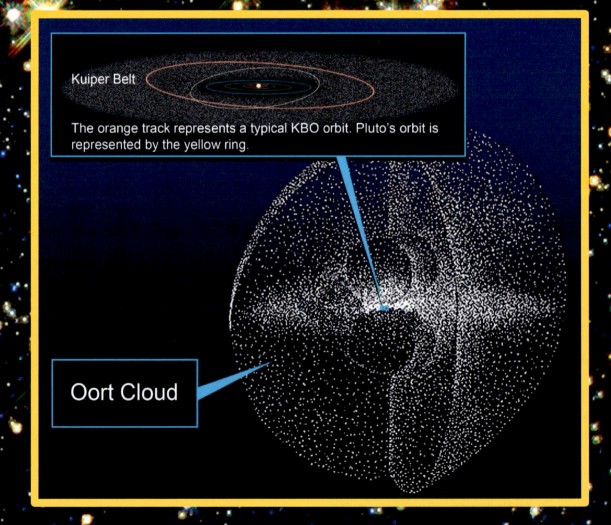

Kuiper Belt

The orange track represents a typical KBO orbit. Pluto's orbit is represented by the yellow ring.

Oort Cloud

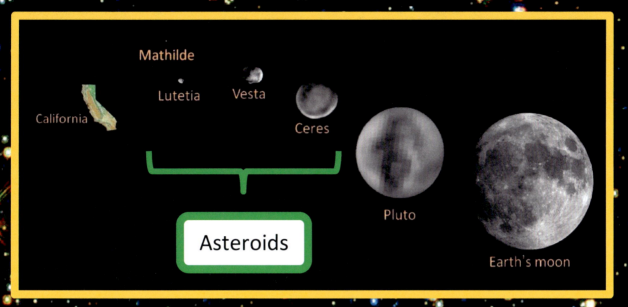

California   Mathilde   Lutetia   Vesta   Ceres   Pluto   Earth's moon

Asteroids

There are countless chunks of rock that are leftovers from the formation of the planets in our solar system, which are called asteroids. Most of the asteroids orbit the sun in the Asteroid Belt between Mars and Jupiter.

The two largest known asteroids are Ceres (Sir-ease) and Vesta.

An asteroid that is heading toward Earth is called a meteoroid while it is still in space.

When it enters Earth's atmosphere, it is called a meteor. We see the meteor because it emits a flash of light as it passes through the atmosphere.

This asteroid has a "moon"!

If part of the meteor reaches the ground (instead of completely burning up), we call the piece that remains a meteorite.

Comet

A comet is an icy body that travels in an elongated elliptical orbit and develops a head and tail as it passes near the sun.

Numerous comets reside in the Kuiper Belt and Oort Cloud.

A comet is often described as a "dirty snowball."

A comet's tail always points directly away from the sun (so it often points sideways, and not backwards, compared to the direction of the comet's velocity). As the nucleus of the comet is heated as it passes near the sun, it creates a visible coma (head) – an atmosphere of gas that comes from heating the ice – and develops a tail (partly formed by gas that escapes from the coma when it is pushed by the solar wind).

This meteorite was found in Antarctica in 1981 and matches rocks gathered from the moon during an Apollo mission.

The two faces of the block showing have the letters E and T – the abbreviation (ET) for extraterrestrial.

The sun lies at the center of our solar system. The planets orbit the sun. From closest to furthest from the sun, the order of the planets is: Mercury, Venus, Earth, Mars, Jupiter, Saturn, Uranus, and Neptune.

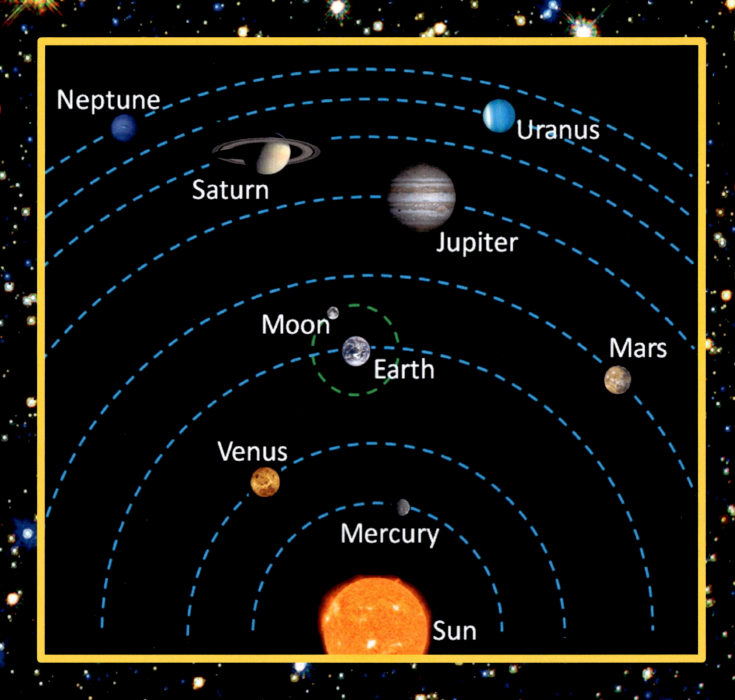

Lunar Phases

New moon: No reflected sunlight is visible; the moon looks completely dark.

Quarter: One-half of the moon appears to be lit by sunlight.

Full moon: Reflected sunlight appears in the shape of a full circle.

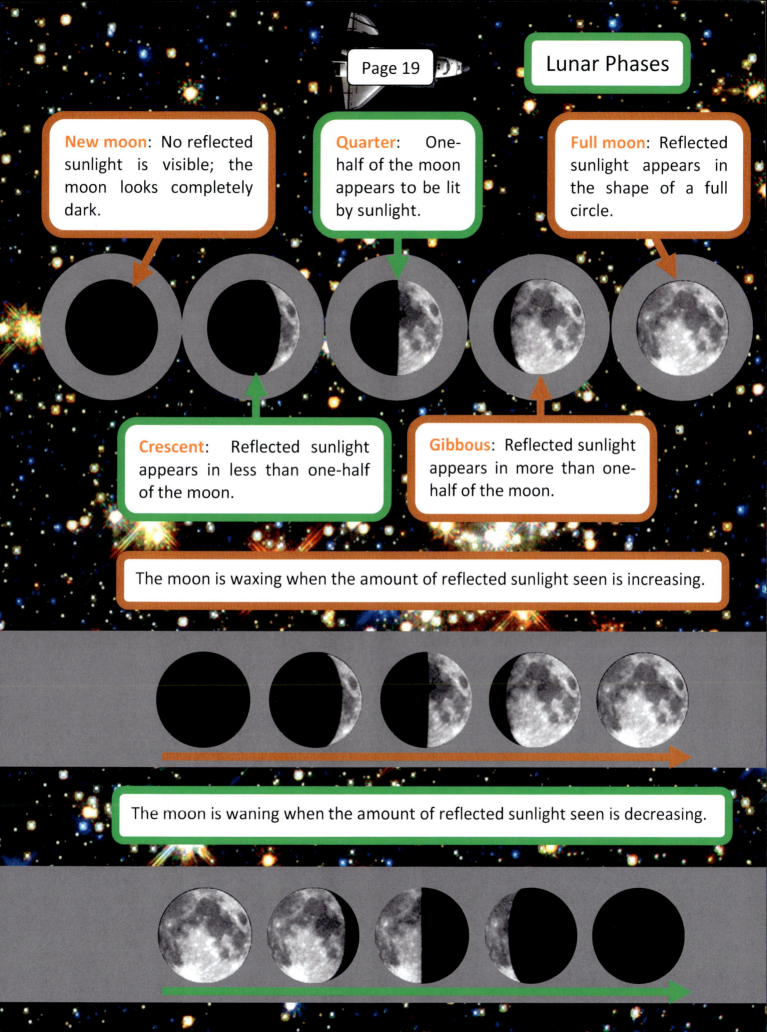

Crescent: Reflected sunlight appears in less than one-half of the moon.

Gibbous: Reflected sunlight appears in more than one-half of the moon.

The moon is waxing when the amount of reflected sunlight seen is increasing.

The moon is waning when the amount of reflected sunlight seen is decreasing.

In the diagram below, a crescent moon is seen from earth. To see this, imagine standing at point A and looking toward the moon. Less than half of the moon would be lit; you would just see a sliver on the right side.

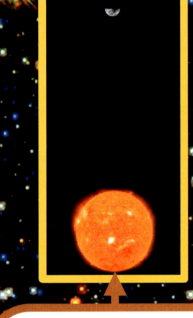

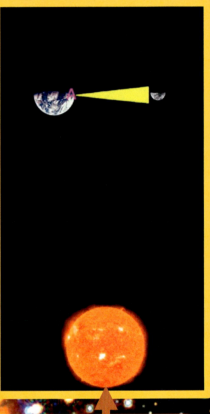

In the diagram above, a new moon is seen from earth. To see this, imagine standing at point A and looking toward the moon. It looks like a solar eclipse, but is not because the moon, earth, and sun do not lie in the same plane when a new moon is formed (to be explained when we discuss eclipses).

In the diagram above, a quarter moon is seen from earth. Sunlight illuminates the moon, and reflected light from the moon is viewed from earth. On earth, the right half of the moon appears lit, while the left half of the moon appears dark. To see this, imagine standing at point A and looking toward the moon.

In this diagram, a gibbous moon is seen from earth. To see this, imagine standing at point A and looking toward the moon. More than half of the moon would be lit.

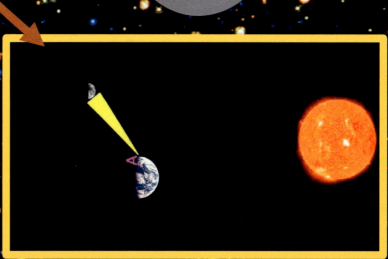

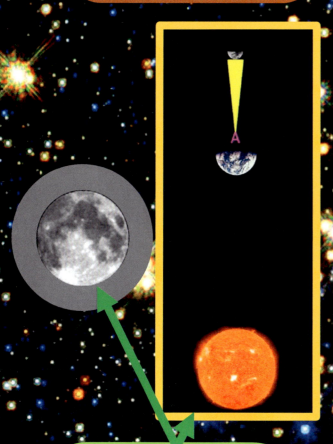

In this diagram, a full moon is seen from earth. To see this, imagine standing at point A and looking toward the moon. It looks like a lunar eclipse, but is not because the moon, earth, and sun do not lie in the same plane when a full moon is formed (to be explained when we discuss eclipses)

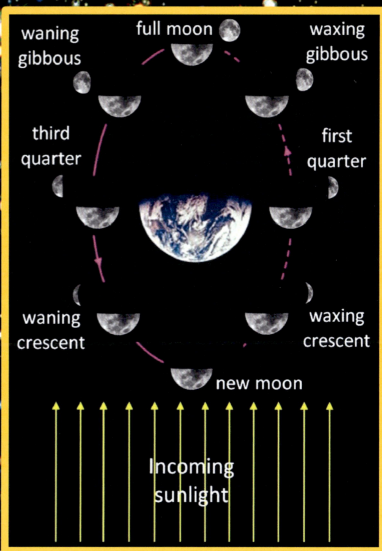

waning gibbous   full moon   waxing gibbous

third quarter   first quarter

waning crescent   waxing crescent

new moon

Incoming sunlight

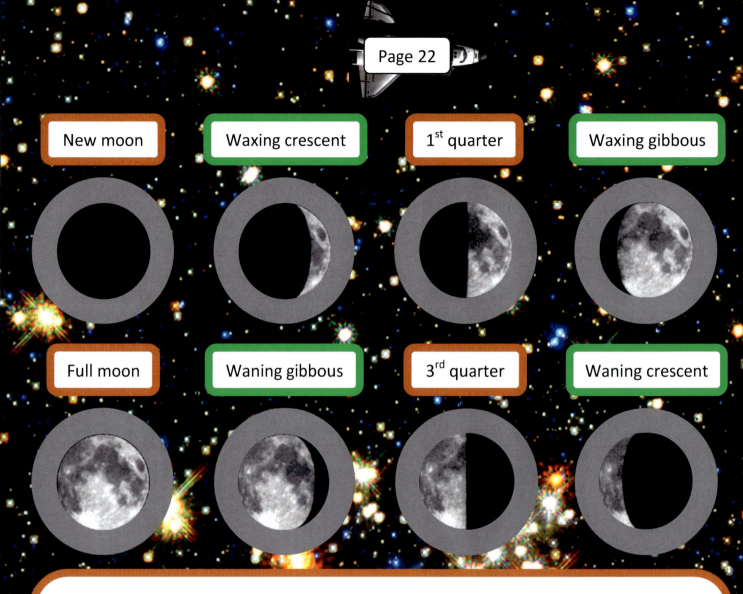

New moon — **Waxing crescent** — **1ˢᵗ quarter** — **Waxing gibbous**

Full moon — **Waning gibbous** — **3ʳᵈ quarter** — **Waning crescent**

The figure on the previous page (bottom right) illustrate how the different phases of the moon – as viewed from earth – are formed. The large moons show the moon's orbit around the earth. The small moons show the phase of the moon as viewed from earth when the moon is in that position. It has to do with the relative positions of the earth, moon, and sun. (It is incorrect to think that the phases of the moon are shadows formed by sunlight that is blocked by the earth.) One-half of the moon is always illuminated by sunlight, but from earth we see every phase from a new moon to a full moon depending on where the moon is in its orbit around the earth.

incoming
sunlight

All of the phases of the lunar cycle, as shown below from left to right, appear in order every 29 and ½ days.

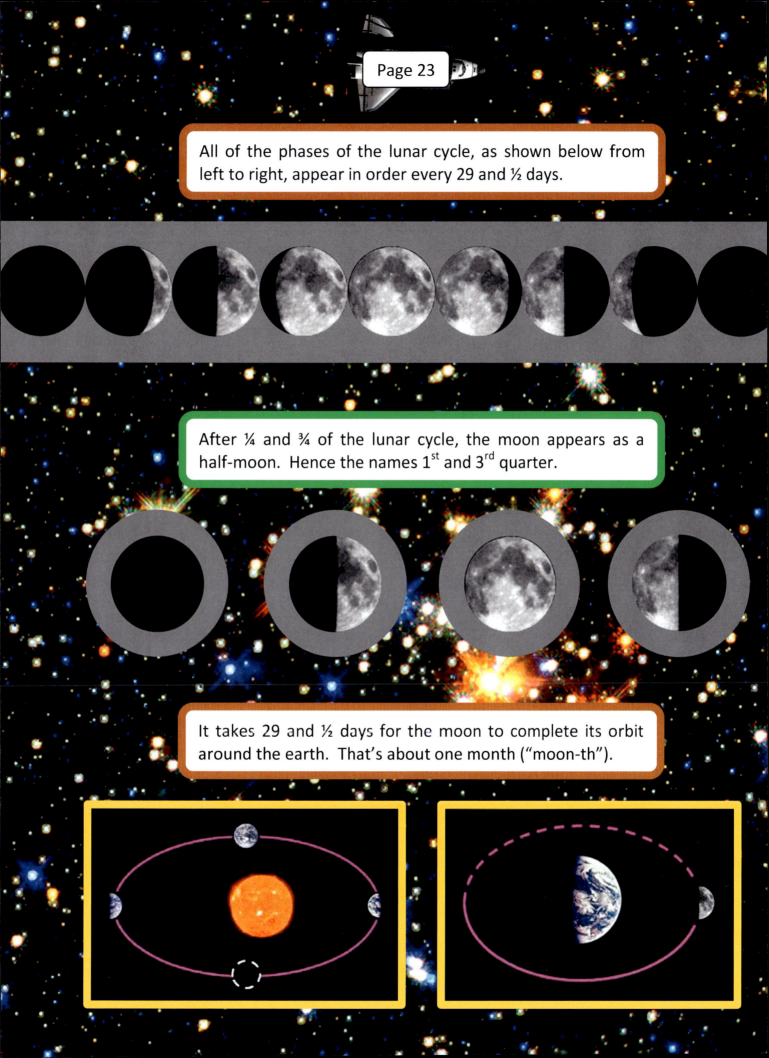

After ¼ and ¾ of the lunar cycle, the moon appears as a half-moon. Hence the names 1st and 3rd quarter.

It takes 29 and ½ days for the moon to complete its orbit around the earth. That's about one month ("moon-th").

Eclipses

shadow on earth

incoming sunlight

new moon position

A solar eclipse occurs when the moon blocks sunlight from reaching earth. When this happens, the moon casts a shadow on earth's surface.

A solar eclipse can only occur during a new moon. However, during most new moons, there is no solar eclipse.

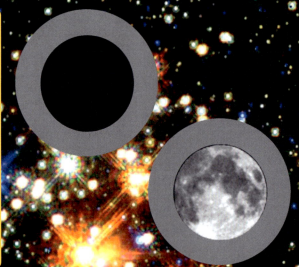

A lunar eclipse occurs when the earth blocks sunlight from reaching the moon. When this happens, the earth casts a shadow on the moon's surface.

A lunar eclipse can only occur during a full moon. However, during most full moons, there is no lunar eclipse.

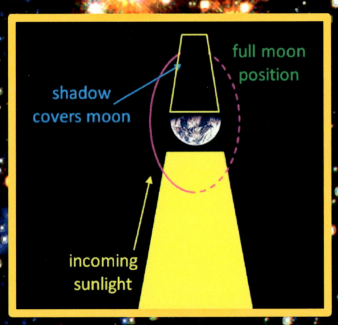

shadow covers moon

full moon position

incoming sunlight

We see a full moon and new moon every month, but solar and lunar eclipses are rare.

The reason that eclipses are rare is that the plane of the moon's orbit around the earth is tilted about 5° compared to the plane of the earth's orbit around the sun. An eclipse can only occur when the moon happens to lie near the plane of the earth's orbit around the sun.

earth-sun plane

moon-earth plane

full moon — it's above the
earth-sun plane, so there is
no lunar eclipse

new moon — it's below the
earth-sun plane, so there is
no solar eclipse

lunar eclipse
the earth, moon, and sun
lie in a line

solar eclipse

lunar eclipse
the earth, moon, and sun
lie in a line

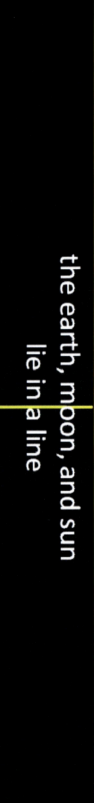

the earth, moon, and sun
lie in a line
lunar eclipse

new moon — it's above the
earth-sun plane, so there is
no solar eclipse

solar eclipse
earth-sun plane,
no solar eclipse

full moon — it's below the
earth-sun plane, so there is
no lunar eclipse

December

incoming sunlight

fewer rays reach a given area

2 points further apart
(more area between 2 rays)

June

incoming sunlight

more rays reach a given area

2 points closer together
(less area between 2 rays)

The intensity of the sunlight equals power per unit area. More rays of sunshine reach a given area of the northern hemisphere in the summer; fewer rays reach a given area in winter.

The tilt of earth's axis (<u>not</u> the earth-sun distance) determines the seasons. Sunlight shines more directly on the northern hemisphere in the summer, so more light reaches a given area of the northern hemisphere's surface; in winter, sunlight enters at an angle such that less light reaches a given area.

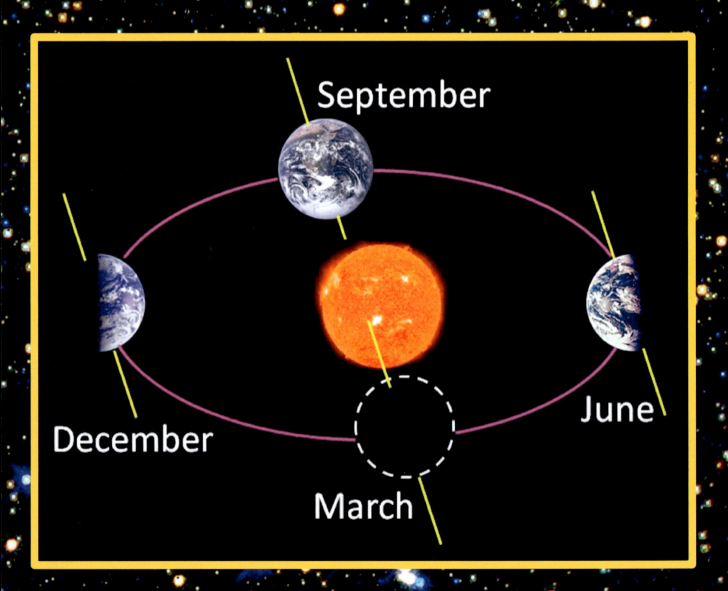

Earth's Shape

For several centuries, sailors have observed that the earth is round. Watch how the boat disappears differently in the two diagrams below.

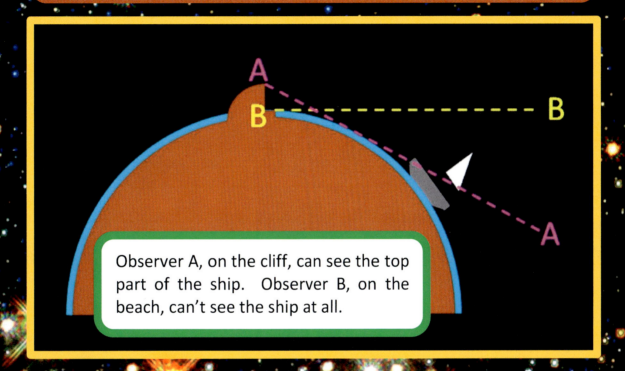

Observer A, on the cliff, can see the top part of the ship. Observer B, on the beach, can't see the ship at all.

Nowadays, we have these convincing space photos from NASA.

Observers A and B see all of the ship. The ship appears smaller as it leaves, but the same proportion of the ship is always visible.

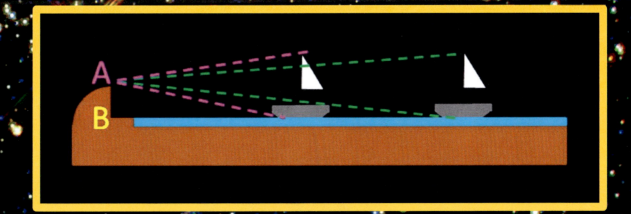

Ptolemy (Tall-uh-me) was a Greek mathematician and librarian who developed a model of our solar system with Earth at the center circa 140 AD. This is called the geocentric model (also known as the Ptolemaic model).

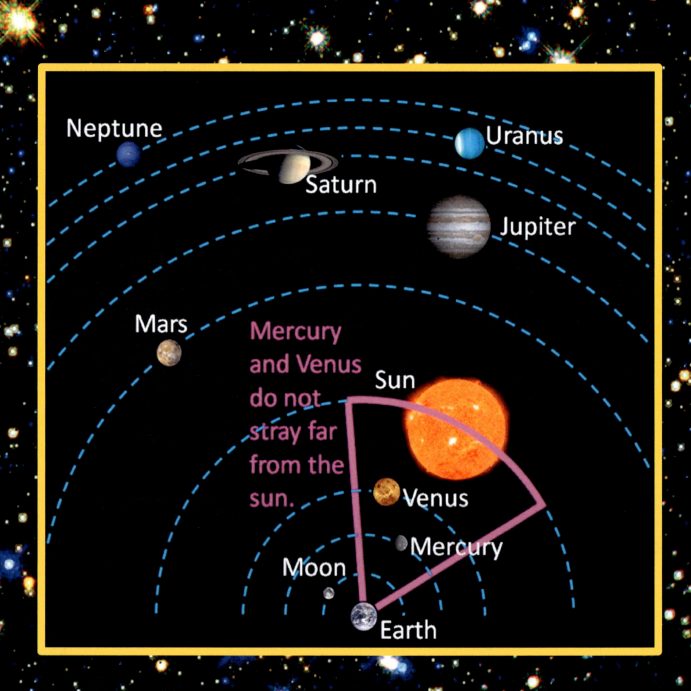

Neptune

Uranus

Saturn

Jupiter

Mars

Mercury and Venus do not stray far from the sun.

Sun

Venus

Mercury

Moon

Earth

Heliocentric Model

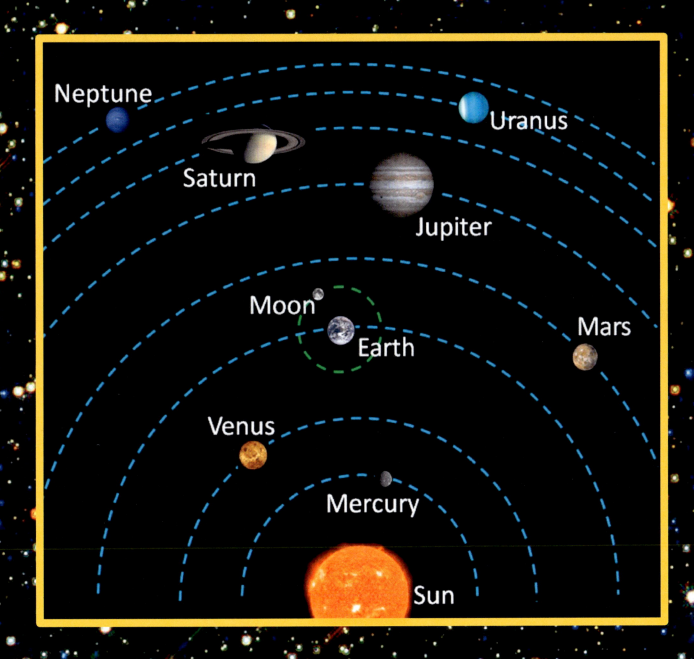

Aristarchus (Are-iss-tar-cuss) was a Greek mathematician who developed a model of our solar system with sun at the center circa 240 BC. This is called the heliocentric model. Nicholas Copernicus (Coe-purr-ni-cuss), who lived from 1473-1543 AD, revived and improved the heliocentric model.

The figure below illustrates retrograde motion (described on the next page) as explained in the heliocentric model. The top right figure shows the retrograde loop observed from earth relative to the fixed stars; the main figure shows earth viewing Mars as earth passes it.

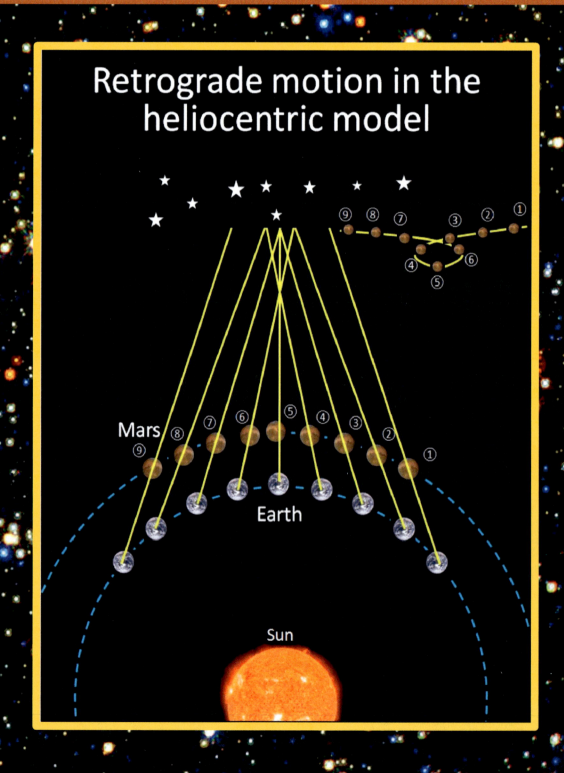

Retrograde motion in the heliocentric model

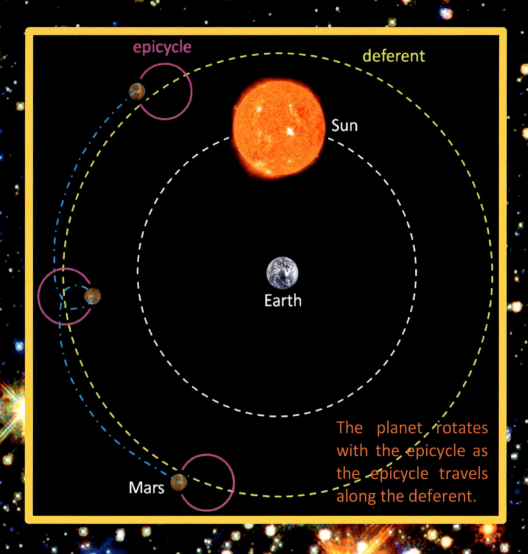

epicycle

deferent

Sun

Earth

Mars

The planet rotates with the epicycle as the epicycle travels along the deferent.

The outer planets usually appear to move in a single direction across the night sky, as viewed from earth. However, when the earth passes an outer planet, for a short period the outer planet appears to move backward. This phenomenon is called retrograde motion.

The figure above illustrates retrograde motion as explained in the geocentric model. The early Greeks introduced the deferent (large circle) and epicycle (small circle) in order to explain retrograde motion.

The Greeks raised some good objections to the heliocentric model:

- If the earth were going around the sun, it would have to move incredibly fast. Why don't all loose objects, like birds and rocks, fall off of the earth? If you run really fast, a loose cap will fall off of your head.
- If the earth were orbiting the sun, it would be an enormous distance from its original position after six months. There should be a parallax shift of nearby stars compared to distant stars as a result of this change in position. Why isn't a very noticeable shift in the positions of the stars observed?

The orbital speed of the earth relative to the sun can be found by dividing earth's circumference ($C = 2\pi R$) by its orbital period (one year). The answer, 30 kilometers per second, is like going from Los Angeles to New York City in 2 minutes!

$$v = \frac{C}{T} = \frac{942{,}000{,}000{,}000 \text{ m}}{31{,}500{,}000 \text{ s}}$$
$$v = 30{,}000 \text{ m/s} = 30 \text{ km/s}$$

$$T = 365 \times 24 \times 60 \times 60$$
$$T = 31{,}500{,}000 \text{ s}$$

$$C = 2\pi R = 2\pi(150{,}000{,}000{,}000 \, m)$$
$$C = 942{,}000{,}000{,}000 \, m$$

Moon
Earth
Sun

- Imagine an airplane flying from Los Angeles to New York City with a box of bananas on its roof. Imagine that the airplane travels with a constant velocity of 30 km/s, so it gets there in about 2 minutes. Do you think the box of bananas would fall off? Why?
- The earth is basically doing to the same thing as it orbits the earth, except for traveling in an ellipse instead of a straight line. What's different about the earth's motion?
- For one, the earth has a significant gravitational field, which attracts all massive objects. Earth is pulling rocks, birds, and all other terrestrial objects toward its center. But imagine the force it would take to prevent a box of bananas from coming off the roof of that airplane at such a high speed!
- For another, there is no air resistance. The earth travels through space. There is no air pushing against it, like there is on the airplane.
- Lastly, Newton's law of inertia explains why objects don't fall off of the earth.

- Isaac Newton (Newt-'n) discovered inertia in the 1600's.
- All objects have inertia, which is a natural tendency to maintain constant velocity.
- Velocity is a combination of speed and direction. Speed means how fast, velocity means how fast and which way.
- All of the objects on the earth have a natural tendency to keep up with the earth. They don't have a natural tendency to fall behind. They don't fall off because they have inertia.
- The box of bananas actually wants to stay on the roof of the airplane because it has inertia. However, the box of bananas would fall off of such a high-speed plane trip because of air resistance.
- The Greeks incorrectly thought that objects had a natural tendency to come to rest. Isaac Newton discovered that moving objects actually have a natural tendency to keep moving. Terrestrial objects come to rest because the force of air resistance overcomes their natural tendency.
- Space is a near-perfect vacuum – it is completely devoid of matter. There is no air or anything else to push objects off the earth. This is why the earth does not slow down, but maintains its speed.

This picture shows the earth in two positions six months apart. Due to earth's change in position, a nearby star appears to shift is position relative to more distant stars. This phenomenon is known as stellar parallax.

You can observe the phenomenon of parallax by placing a finger a foot before your eyes. Close one eye, then the other, and your finger will appear to shift positions.

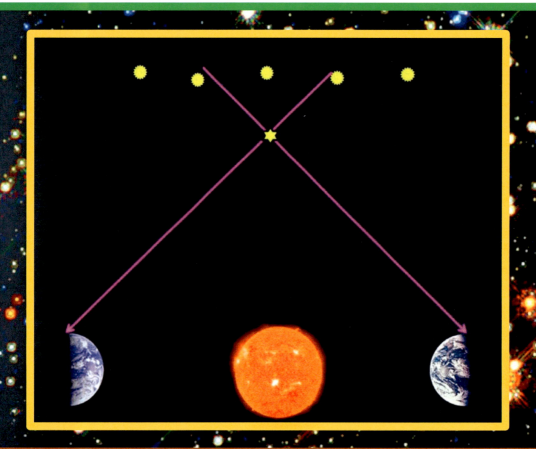

Stellar parallax is actually a very subtle effect, unlike the previous picture, because the earth-sun distance is very tiny compared to the distance to any stars. Stellar parallax can be observed as a very tiny shift, but it requires precise measurements with telescopes. The Greeks did not observe this.

The Greeks didn't imagine that the nearest star could actually be four light-years away. Thus, when they didn't observe a noticeable stellar parallax, they incorrectly concluded that the earth doesn't orbit the sun.

The Modern Heliocentric Model

- The apparent motion of the sun across earth's sky can be explained by earth's rotation on its axis, with the sun stationary.
- The fact that Mercury and Venus can only be seen near the horizon is naturally explained in the heliocentric model: Inner planets can't stray far from the sun.
- The epicycle motion is not needed to explain retrograde motion. This was an unnecessary complication introduced to try to preserve the incorrect geocentric model.
- The stars are so far away that stellar parallax is too small to notice without a telescope.

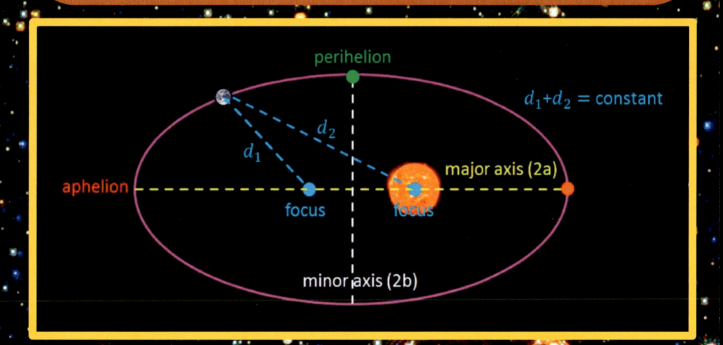

- Tycho Brahe (Tea-co Bra-uh), who lived from 1546 to 1601 AD, built an observatory and made the most accurate astronomical measurements of his day. Tycho was later assisted by Johannes Kepler (Yo-hahn-us Kep-ler), who lived from 1571 to 1630 AD.
- When Kepler compared the astronomical data to Ptolemy's geocentric model and Copernicus' heliocentric model, he realized that (1) the geocentric model is incorrect and (2) the heliocentric model needed to be revised in order to explain the data.
- The necessary revision was to allow the planets to travel in elliptical orbits, rather than circles, with the sun lying at one focus.

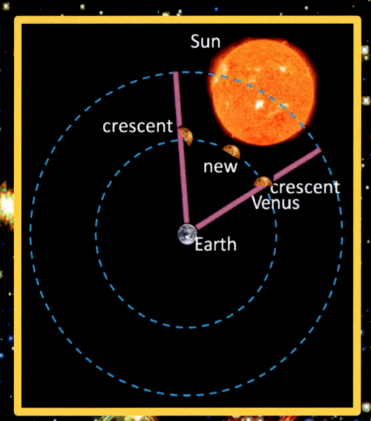

Mercury and Venus are only seen near the horizon from earth. In order to agree with this observation, Mercury and Venus are restricted to lie near the sun in the geocentric model. Venus can only be new or a crescent in the geocentric model. Venus can't be a gibbous or full in the geocentric model.

All of the phases of Venus, from new to full, are possible in the heliocentric model. Galileo (Gal-uh-lay-oh) Galilee, who lived from 1564-1642, observed a full phase of Venus through a telescope. This evidence supports the heliocentric model and rules out the geocentric model.

- Our solar system is heliocentric, <u>not</u> geocentric. That is, the Earth revolves around the sun; the sun does <u>not</u> revolve around the Earth. We know that the solar system is sun-centered and <u>not</u> Earth-centered because we have observed a full Venus through a telescope, which is only possible in the heliocentric model.
- The order of the planets from the sun is Mercury, Venus, Earth, Mars, Jupiter, Saturn, Uranus, and Neptune. Pluto is now considered to be one of several dwarf planets and one of numerous Kuiper Belt objects instead of a planet.
- The Earth rotates on its (tilted) axis once every 24 hours (one rotation). The Earth orbits the sun every 365 days (one revolution).
- The tilt of Earth's axis causes the seasons.
- The Earth is shaped like a sphere. It is round, <u>not</u> flat. We know that the Earth is round from observations of sailing ships, measurements of shadows cast by the sun, and photographs taken from space.
- The moon orbits the Earth every 29.5 days. The phases of the moon are caused by the ever-changing positions of the moon and sun relative to the Earth. They are <u>not</u> caused by shadows of the Earth cast on the moon.
- A solar eclipse occurs when the moon blocks sunlight from reaching the Earth, while a lunar eclipse occurs when the Earth blocks sunlight from reaching the moon. Eclipses are rare because the moon's orbit is tilted compared to the Earth's orbit.

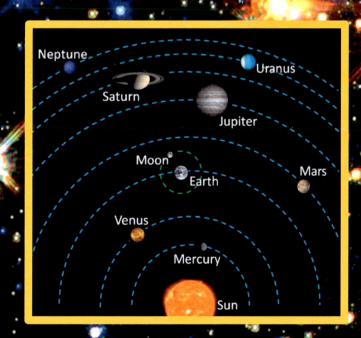

The author, Chris McMullen, is a physics and astronomy instructor at Northwestern State University of Louisiana. He earned his Ph.D. in physics at Oklahoma State University in phenomenological high-energy physics (particle physics). His doctoral dissertation was on the collider phenomenology of superstring-inspired large extra dimensions, a field in which he has coauthored several papers.

Made in the USA
San Bernardino, CA
02 March 2018